PIANO | VOCAL | GUITAR • AUDIO   VOLUME 128

HAL•LEONARD®
PIANO PLAY-ALONG

AUDIO
ACCESS
INCLUDED

Frozen

T0065953

CONTENTS

To access audio visit:
www.halleonard.com/mylibrary

Enter Code
4400-9108-6012-9480

Audio Arrangements by Peter Deneff

ISBN 978-1-4803-8644-0

Disney characters and artwork © Disney Enterprises, Inc.

WONDERLAND MUSIC COMPANY, INC.

DISTRIBUTED BY

7777 W. BLUEMOUND RD. P.O. BOX 13819 MILWAUKEE, WI 53213

In Australia Contact:
Hal Leonard Australia Pty. Ltd.
4 Lentara Court
Cheltenham, Victoria, 3192 Australia
Email: ausadmin@halleonard.com.au

Visit Hal Leonard Online at
www.halleonard.com

DO YOU WANT TO BUILD A SNOWMAN?

Music and Lyrics by KRISTEN ANDERSON-LOPEZ
and ROBERT LOPEZ

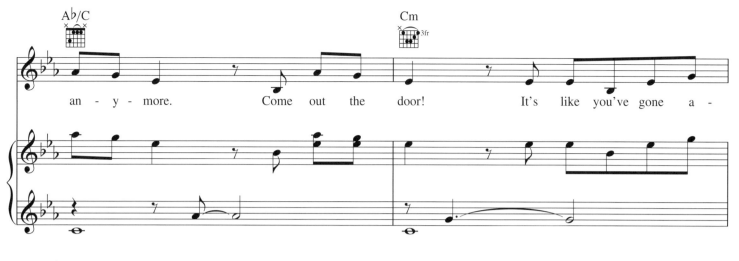

an - y - more. Come out the door! It's like you've gone a -

way. We used to be best bud - dies, and

now we're not. ___ I wish you would tell me why.

Do you want to build a snow - man? It does - n't have to be a

snow - man. **LITTLE ELSA:** *(Spoken:) Go away, Anna.* **LITTLE ANNA:** *(Sung:)* O - kay,

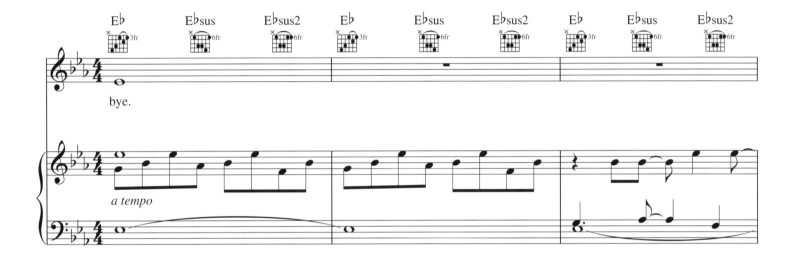

bye.

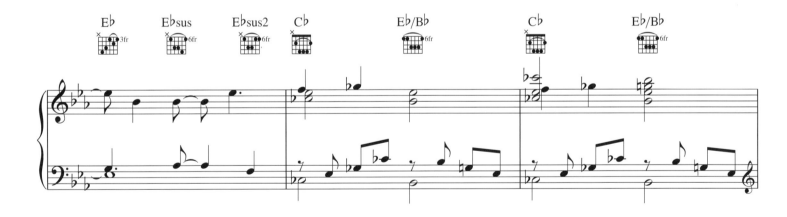

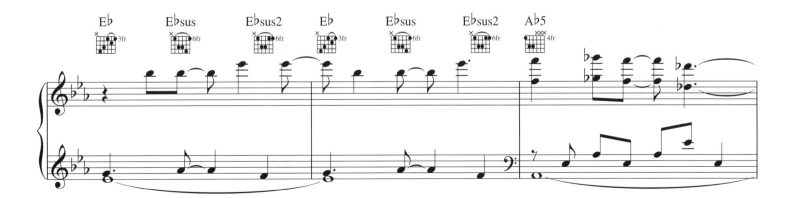

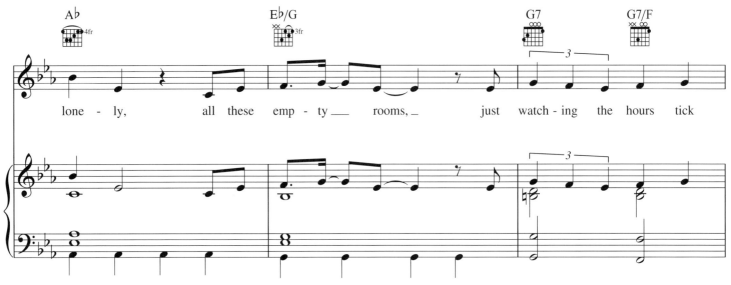

lone - ly, all these emp - ty ___ rooms, ___ just watch - ing the hours tick

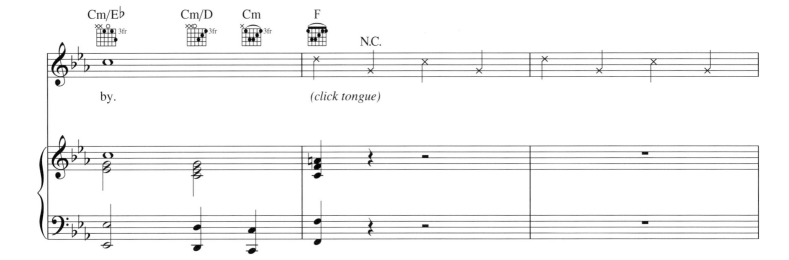

by.

(click tongue)

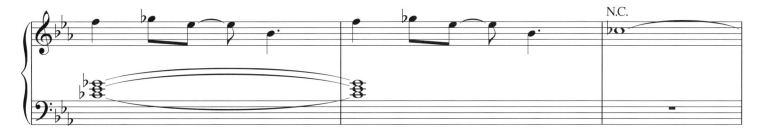

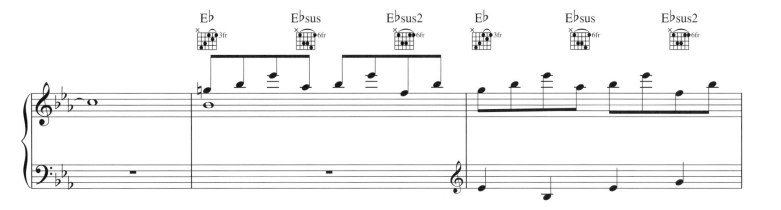

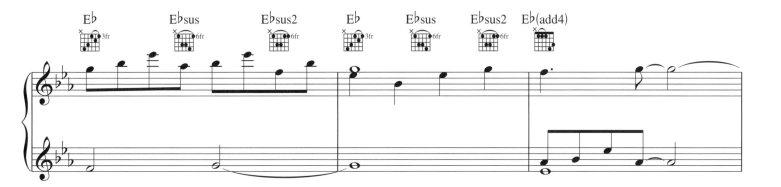

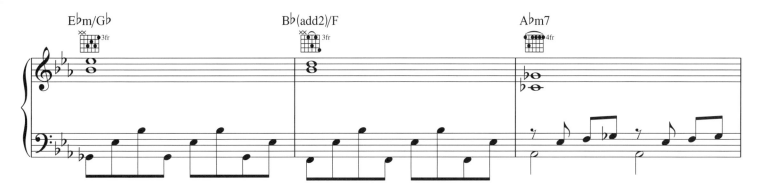

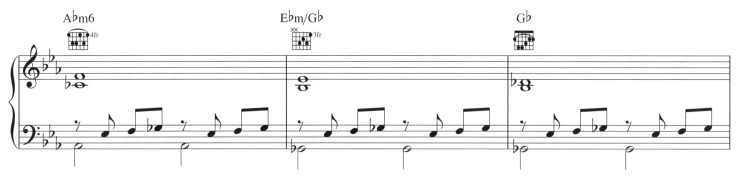

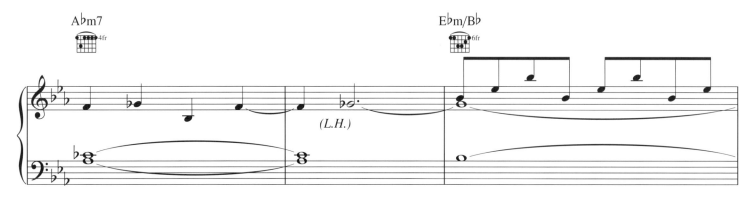

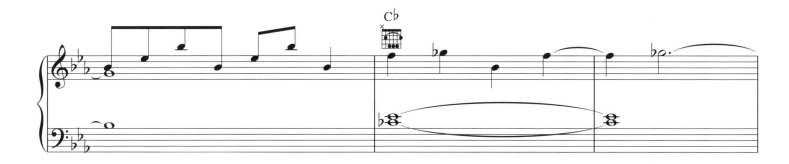

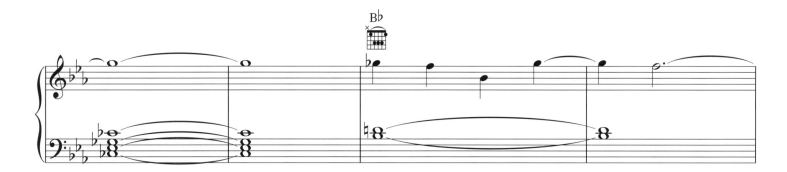

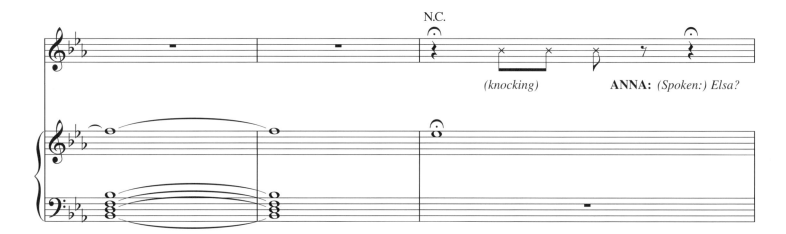

(knocking)

ANNA: *(Spoken:) Elsa?*

A little slower, tenderly

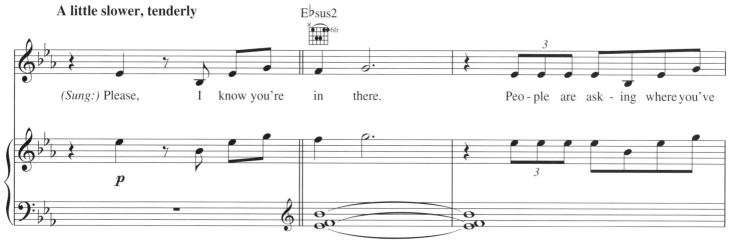

(Sung:) Please, I know you're in there. Peo-ple are ask-ing where you've

been. They say, "Have cour-age," and I'm

try-ing to; I'm right out here for you, just let me in.

We on-ly have each oth-er; it's just you and me.

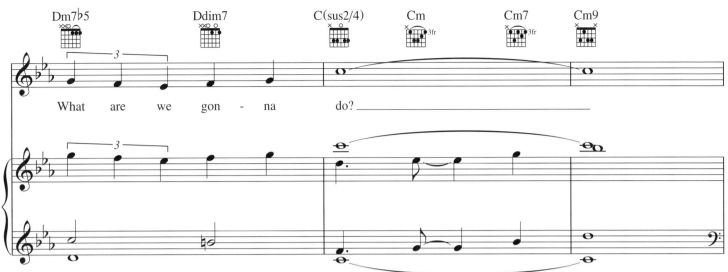

What are we gon - na do? _____

Do you want to build a snow - man?

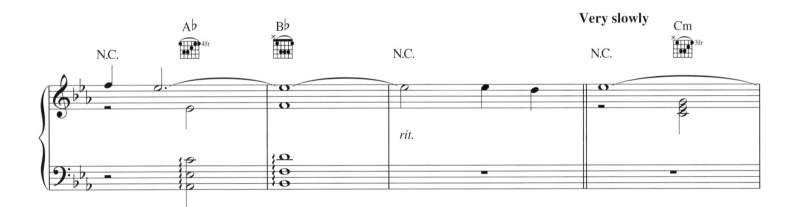

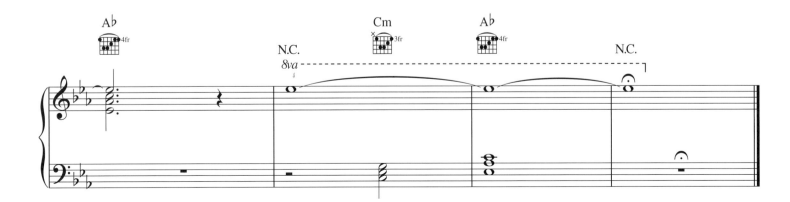

IN SUMMER

Music and Lyrics by KRISTEN ANDERSON-LOPEZ
and ROBERT LOPEZ

lax - ing in the sum-mer sun, _ just let - tin' off steam. _ Oh, the

Slower

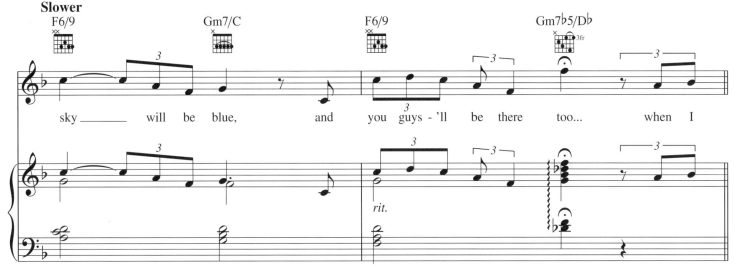

sky _____ will be blue, and you guys - 'll be there too... when I

Tempo I

fi - nal - ly do what fro - zen things do in sum - mer. _____

KRISTOFF: *(Spoken:)*
I'm gonna tell him.

Very broadly

ANNA: *(Spoken:)*
Don't you dare!

(Sung:) In sum - mer! _____

FIXER UPPER

Music and Lyrics by KRISTEN ANDERSON-LOPEZ
and ROBERT LOPEZ

With comic bounce

BULDA: *(Spoken:) What's the issue, dear? Why are you holding back from such a man?* *(Sung:)* Is it the

clump-y way __ he walks? **CLIFF:** Or the grump-y way __ he talks? Or the

pear-shaped, square-shaped weird-ness of his feet? **MALE TROLL 1:** And though we

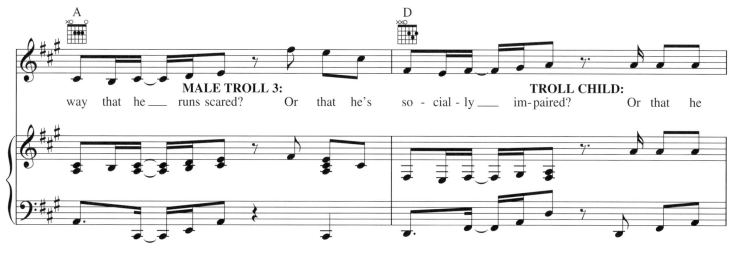

MALE TROLL 3: way that he ___ runs scared? Or that he's so - cial - ly ___ im-paired? **TROLL CHILD:** Or that he

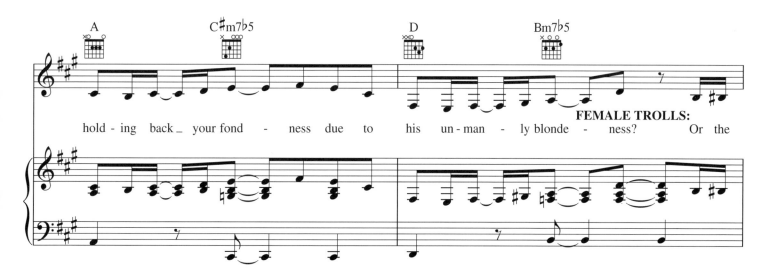

on - ly likes ___ to tin - kle in ___ the woods? *(Spoken:) What?* **CLIFF:** *(Sung:)* Are you

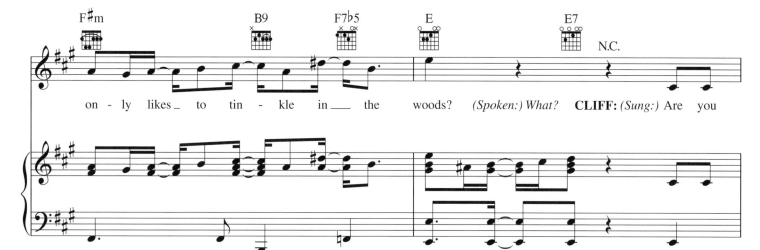

hold - ing back ___ your fond - ness due to his un - man - ly blonde - ness? **FEMALE TROLLS:** Or the

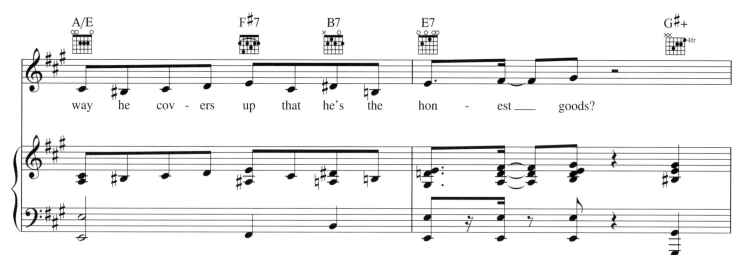

way he cov - ers up that he's the hon - est ___ goods?

ALL TROLLS:
He's just a bit of a fix- er up- per; he's got a cou-ple 'a bugs. ___ His
i- so- la- tion is con- fir- ma- tion of his des-per-a- tion for heal-ing hugs! ___
So he's a bit of a fix- er up- per, but we know what ___ to do: ___ the
way to fix up this fix- er up- per is to fix him up ___ with you!

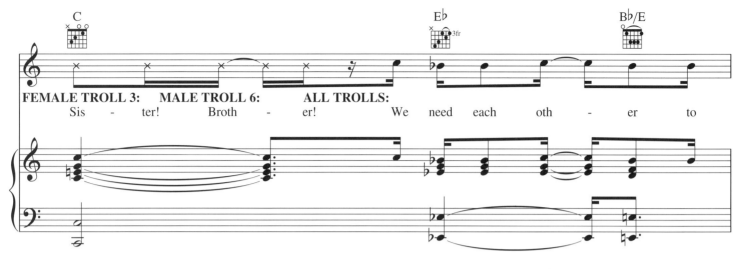

FEMALE TROLL 3: Sis - ter! **MALE TROLL 6:** Broth - er! **ALL TROLLS:** We need each oth - er to

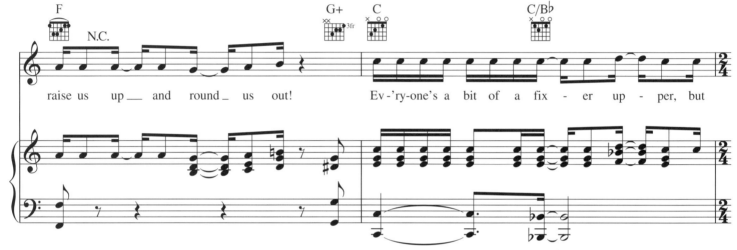

raise us up ___ and round ___ us out! Ev - 'ry-one's a bit of a fix - er up - per, but

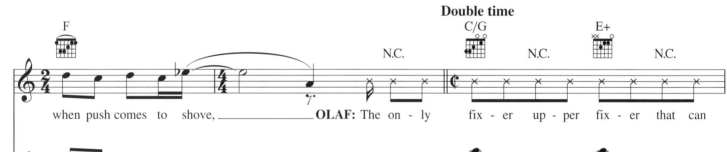

Double time

when push comes to shove, _____ **OLAF:** The on - ly fix - er up - per fix - er that can

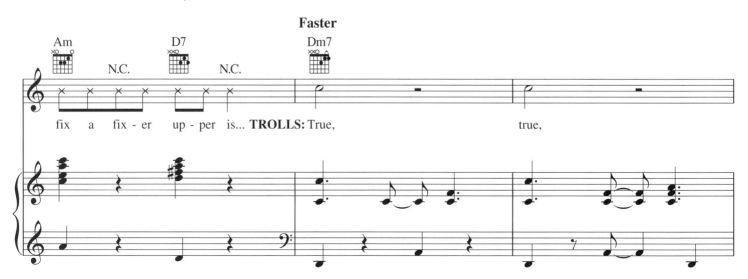

Faster

fix a fix - er up - per is... **TROLLS:** True,   true,

FOR THE FIRST TIME IN FOREVER

Music and Lyrics by KRISTEN ANDERSON-LOPEZ
and ROBERT LOPEZ

With excitement

With pedal

ANNA: The win-dow is o - pen! So's _ that door! _ I

did-n't know they did that an - y - more. _ Who knew we owned _ eight thou - sand sal - ad

plates?

For years I've roamed _ these emp - ty halls. _

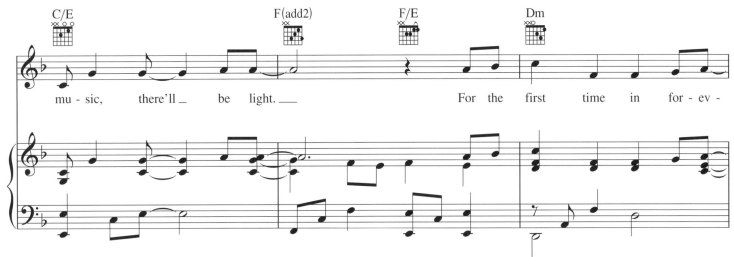

music, there'll _ be light. _ For the first time in for- ev-

-er, I'll be danc- ing through _ the night. _ Don't

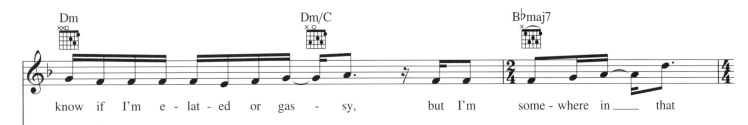

know if I'm e- lat- ed or gas - sy, but I'm some- where in ___ that

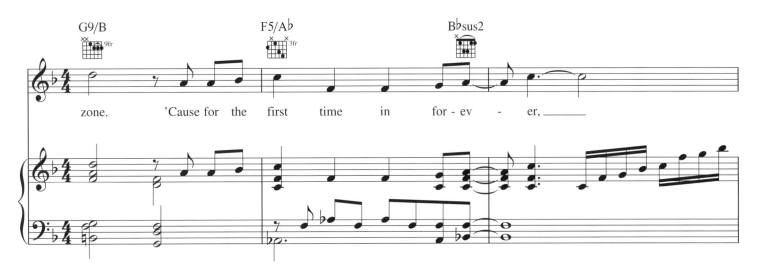

zone. 'Cause for the first time in for- ev- er, _____

Excited again

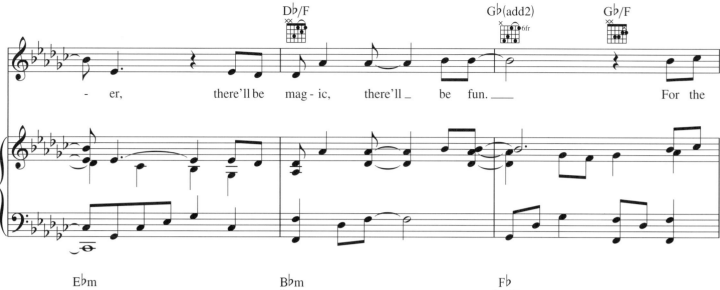

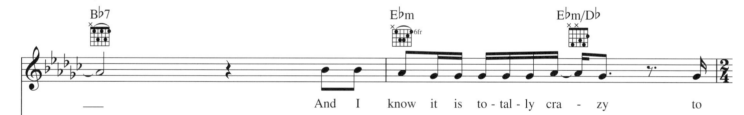

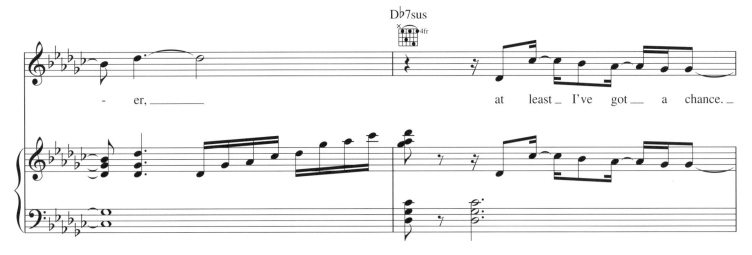

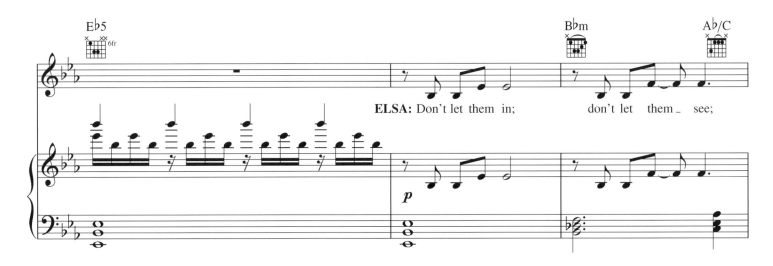

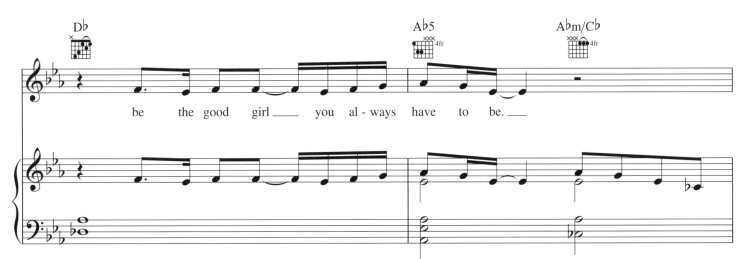

LET IT GO

Music and Lyrics by KRISTEN ANDERSON-LOPEZ
and ROBERT LOPEZ

Half-time feel, mysterious

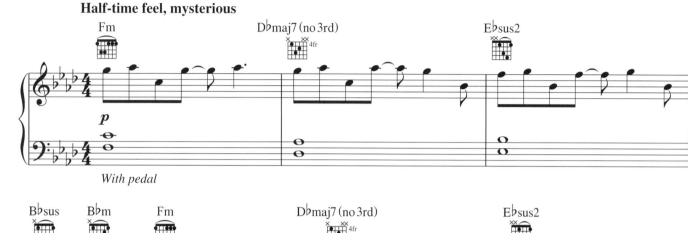

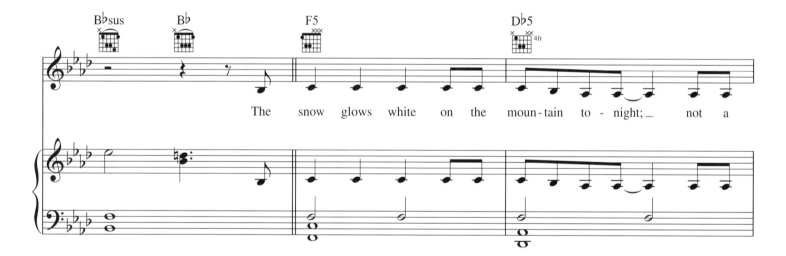

The snow glows white on the moun-tain to-night; __ not a

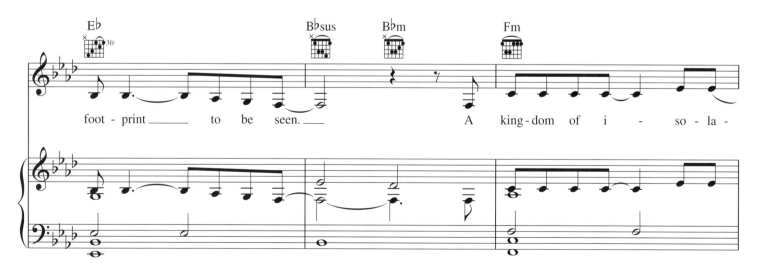

foot-print _____ to be seen. ___ A king-dom of i - so - la -

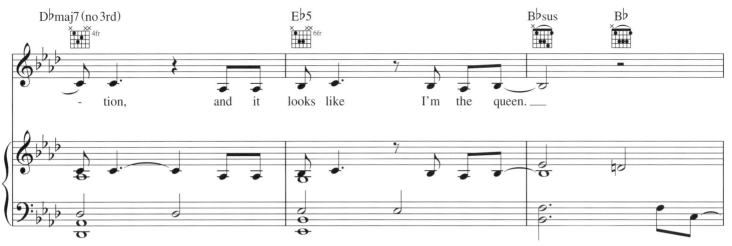

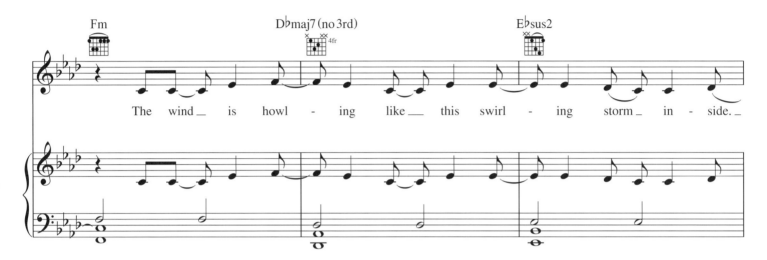

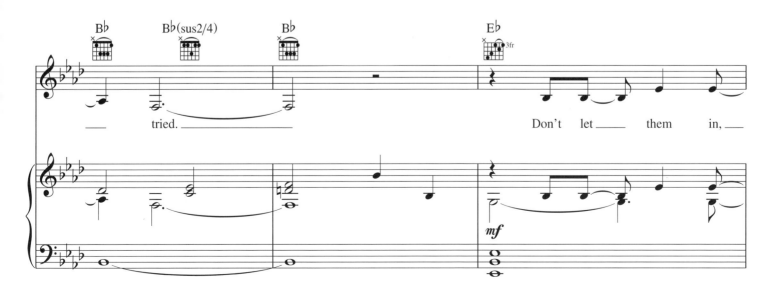

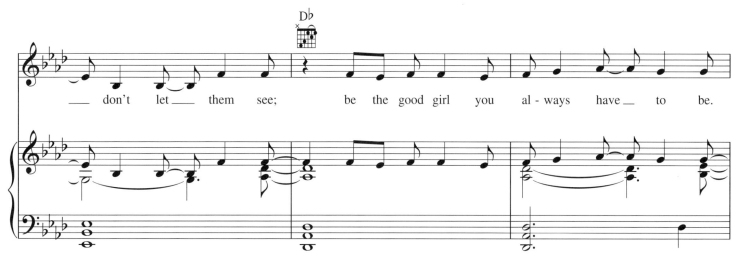

don't let them see; be the good girl you al-ways have to be.

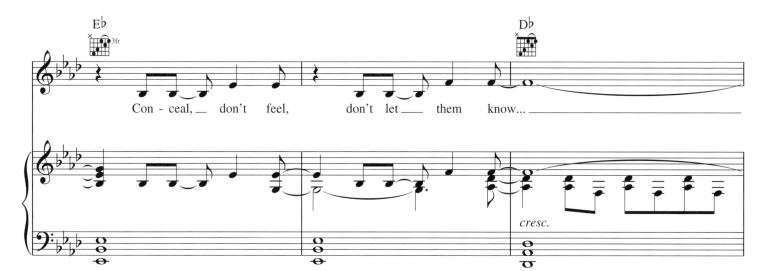

Con-ceal, don't feel, don't let them know...

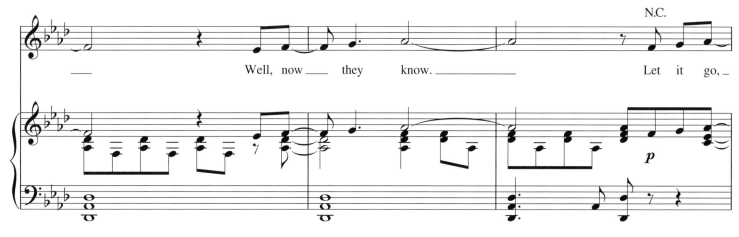

Well, now they know. Let it go,

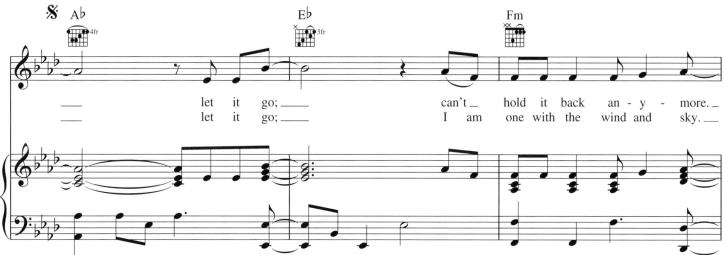

let it go; can't hold it back an-y-more.
let it go; I am one with the wind and sky.

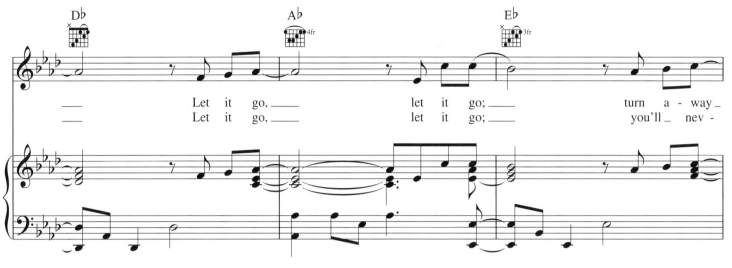

Let it go, _____ let it go; _____ turn a - way_
Let it go, _____ let it go; _____ you'll_ nev -

_____ and slam _____ the _____ door. _____ I _____ don't _____ care _____
- er see me _____ cry. _____ Here _____ I _____ stand, _

_____ what they're going to _____ say; _____ let the
_____ and going here I'll _____ stay; _____ let the

To Coda

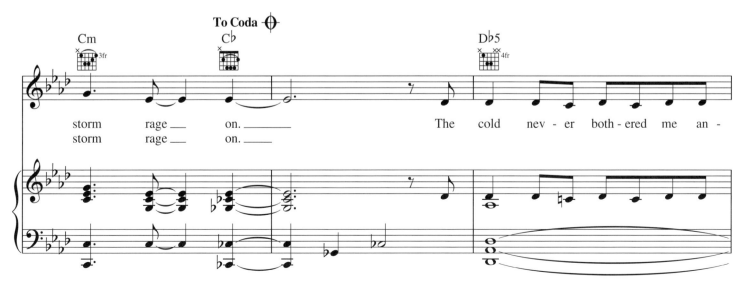

storm rage _____ on. _____ The cold nev - er both - ered me an -
storm rage _____ on. _____

Gaining confidence

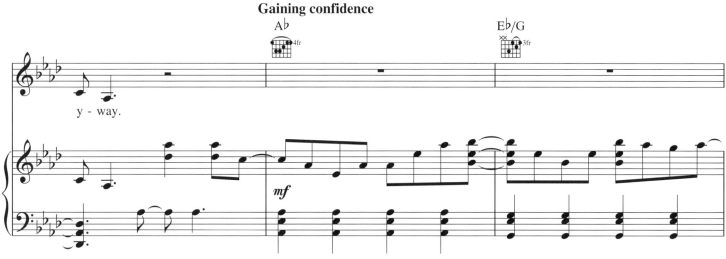

y - way.

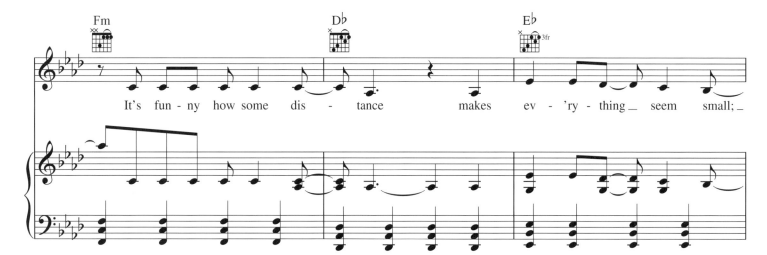

It's fun-ny how some dis - tance makes ev - 'ry-thing __ seem small; __

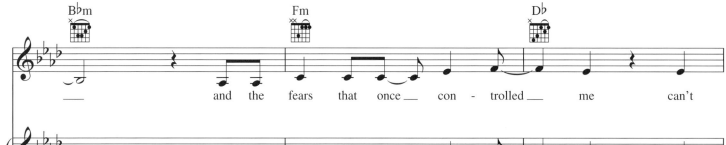

__ and the fears that once __ con - trolled __ me can't

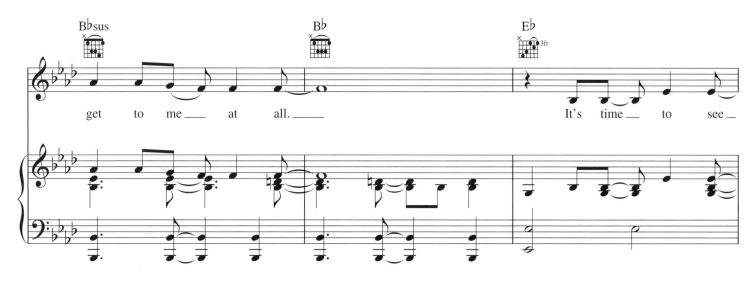

get to me __ at all. __ It's time __ to see __

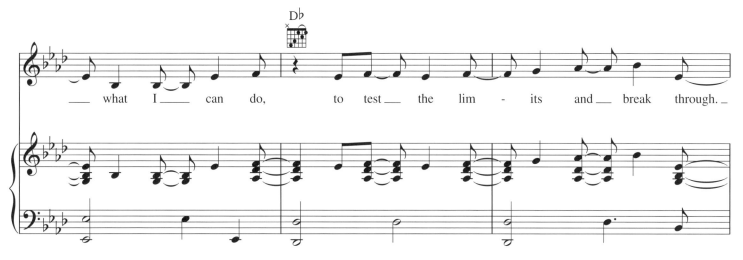

My pow - er flur - ries through _ the air _

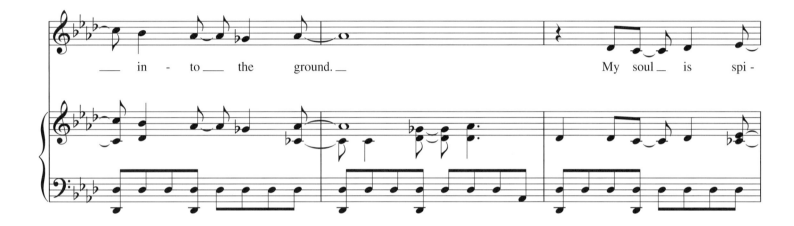

_ in - to _ the ground. _ My soul _ is spi -

- ral - ing _ in fro - zen frac - tals all _ a - round. _

Eb5
N.C.

And one _ thought cry - stal - li - zes like _ an i - cy blast: _

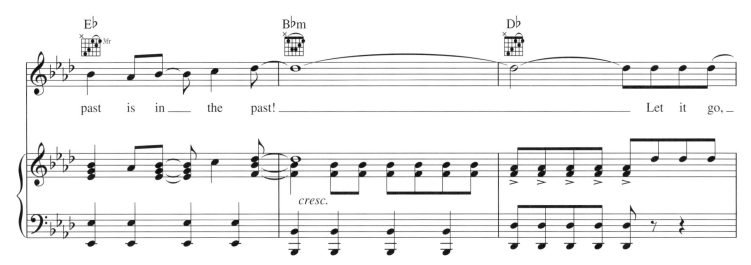

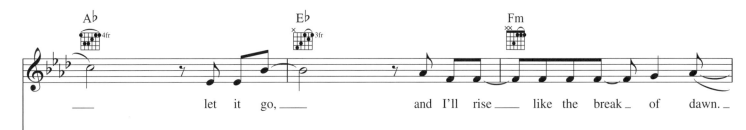

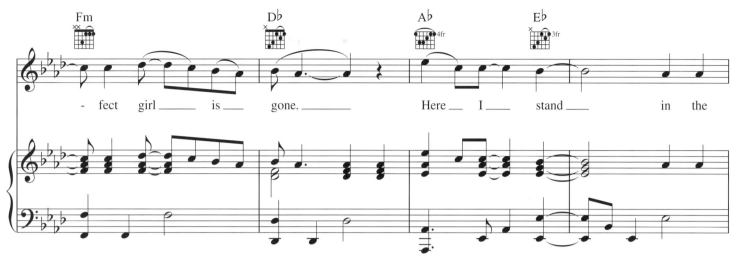

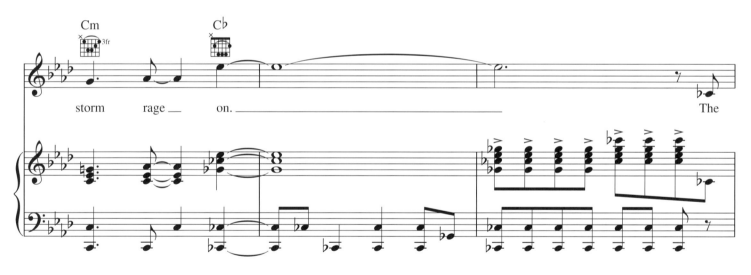

REINDEER(S) ARE BETTER THAN PEOPLE

Music and Lyrics by KRISTEN ANDERSON-LOPEZ
and ROBERT LOPEZ

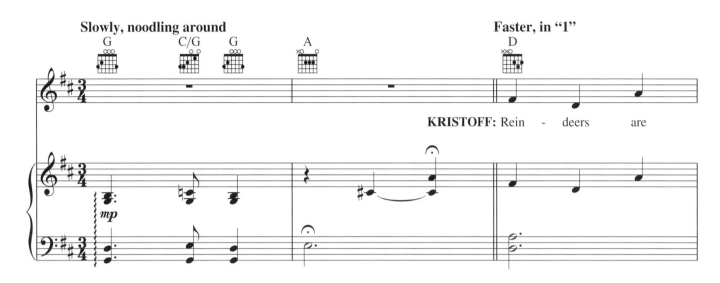

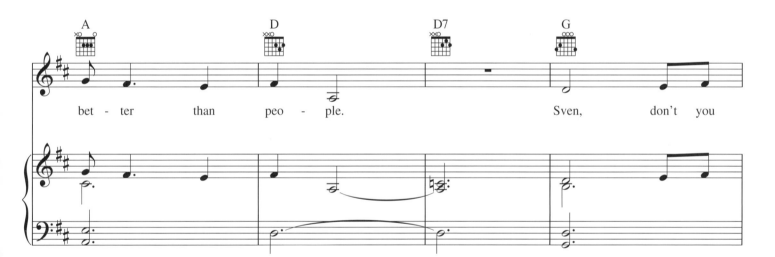

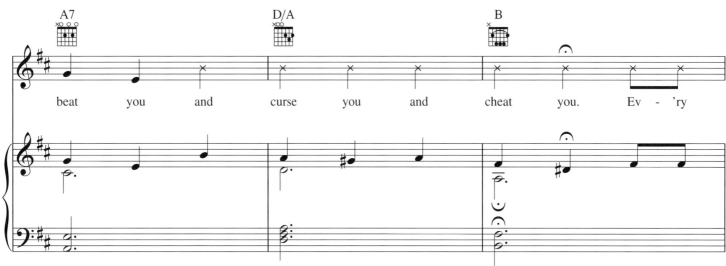

beat you and curse you and cheat you. Ev - 'ry

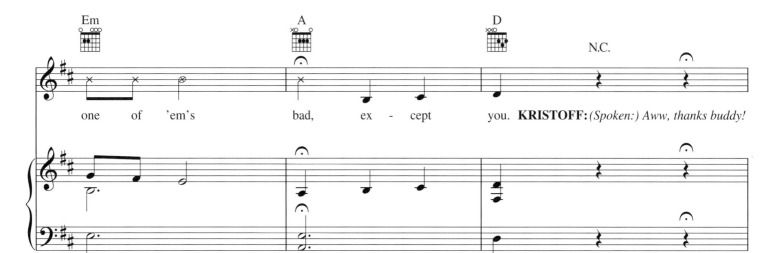

one of 'em's bad, ex - cept you. **KRISTOFF:** *(Spoken:) Aww, thanks buddy!*

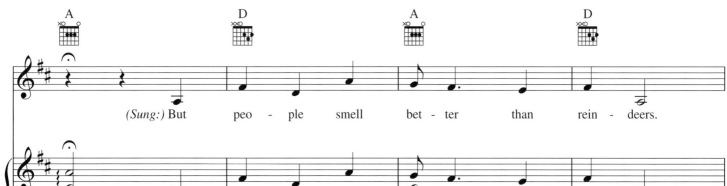

(Sung:) But peo - ple smell bet - ter than rein - deers.

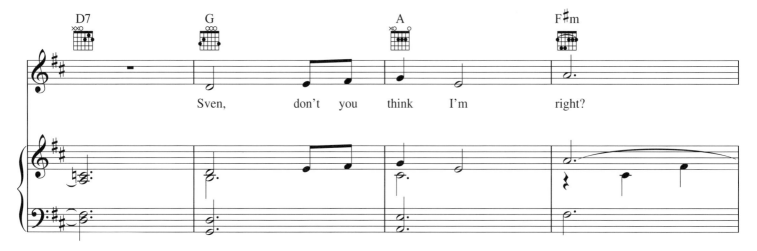

Sven, don't you think I'm right?

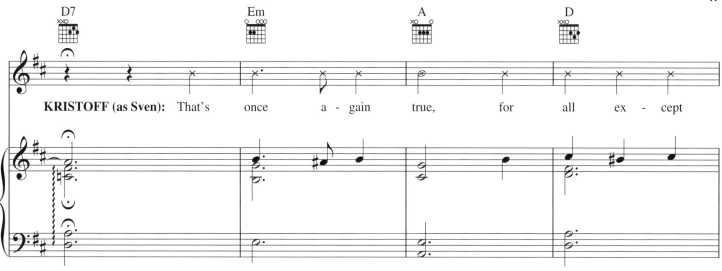

KRISTOFF (as Sven): That's once a - gain true, for all ex - cept

you. KRISTOFF: You got me! Let's call it a

night. KRISTOFF (as Sven): Good - night! KRISTOFF: Don't let the

Slower

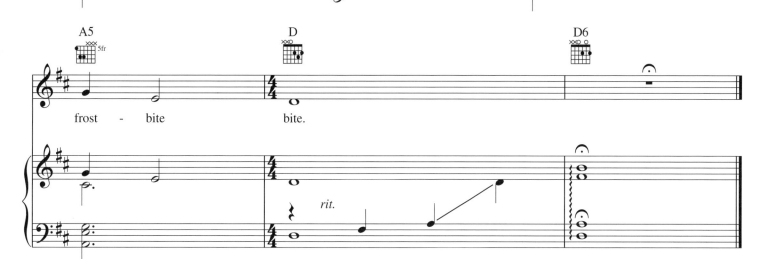

frost - bite bite.

rit.

LOVE IS AN OPEN DOOR

Music and Lyrics by KRISTEN ANDERSON-LOPEZ
and ROBERT LOPEZ

I see your face, and it's noth-ing like ___ I've ev-er known ___ be-

___ place. and it's noth-ing like ___ I've ev-er known ___ be-

fore. Love is an o - pen door. ___

fore. Love is an o - pen door. ___

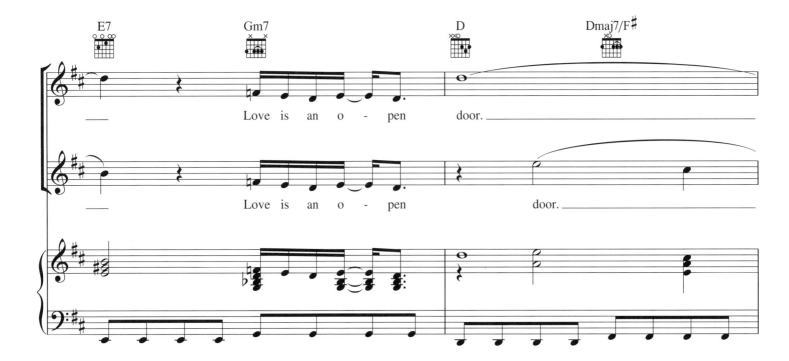

___ Love is an o - pen door. ___

___ Love is an o - pen door. ___

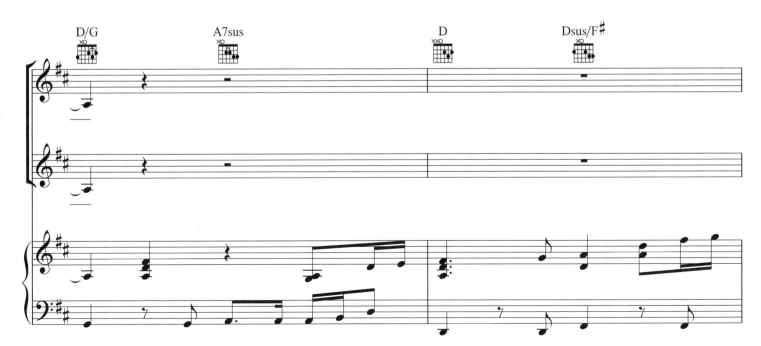

THE ULTIMATE SONGBOOKS

HAL•LEONARD®
PIANO PLAY-ALONG

AUDIO ACCESS INCLUDED

These great songbook/audio packs come with our standard arrangements for piano and voice with guitar chord frames plus audio.

The audio includes a full performance of each song, as well as a second track without the piano part so you can play "lead" with the band! Volumes 86 and beyond also include the Amazing Slow Downer technology so PC and Mac users can adjust the recording to any tempo without changing the pitch! Packs include CDs unless otherwise marked.

HAL•LEONARD®
CORPORATION
7777 W. BLUEMOUND RD. P.O. BOX 13819
MILWAUKEE, WISCONSIN 53213

Visit Hal Leonard Online at
www.halleonard.com